D1449298

A Life in the Theatre

OTHER WORKS BY DAVID MAMET

American Buffalo
Sexual Perversity in Chicago and *The Duck Variations*

A Life in the Theatre

A PLAY BY
David Mamet

GROVE PRESS, INC./NEW YORK

THIS PLAY IS DEDICATED TO
Gregory Mosher

We counterfeited once for your disport
Men's joy and sorrow; but our day has passed.
We pray you pardon all where we fell short—
Seeing we were your servants to this last.

Rudyard Kipling,

Actors

The Characters

ROBERT   An older actor

JOHN   A younger actor

The Scene

Various spots around a theatre.

The scenes in this play can be divided into onstage and backstage scenes. In the onstage scenes, we see JOHN and ROBERT portraying characters in various plays in the repertory theatre for which they work. A beautiful solution for staging *A Life in the Theatre* in a proscenium house was arrived at by Michael Merritt and Gregory Mosher, the play's first designer and director, respectively, in their production at the Goodman Theatre Stage Two, in Chicago. They decided that it might be provocative if a second curtain were installed upstage, behind which the audience for whom JOHN and ROBERT play their onstage scenes sits. This curtain is opened when JOHN and ROBERT work onstage, which is to say, playing in a play. Thus we see the actors' backs during their onstage scenes, and a full view of them during the backstage scenes—in effect, a true view from backstage.

A Life in the Theatre was first produced by the Theatre de Lys, New York City, and opened on October 20, 1977, with the following cast:

JOHN   Peter Evans

ROBERT   Ellis Rabb

STAGE MANAGER   Benjamin Hendrickson

The production was directed by Gerald Gutierrez; set by John Lee Beatty; lighting by Pat Collins.

The New York production of *A Life in the Theatre* included a silent character, the STAGE MANAGER.

Scene 1

Backstage, after a performance.

ROBERT: Goodnight, John.

JOHN: Goodnight.

ROBERT: I thought the bedroom scene tonight was brilliant.

JOHN: Did you?

ROBERT: Yes, I did. (*Pause.*) Didn't you think it went well?

    JOHN *shrugs.*

ROBERT: Well, I thought it went brilliantly.

JOHN: Thank you.

ROBERT: I wouldn't tell you if it wasn't so.

    Pause.

JOHN: Thank you.

ROBERT: Not at all. I wouldn't say it if it weren't so.

JOHN: The show went well tonight.

ROBERT: I think it did.

JOHN: They were very bright.

ROBERT: Yes. They were.

JOHN: It was . . .

    Pause.

ROBERT: What?

JOHN: An intelligent house. Didn't you feel?

ROBERT: I did.

JOHN: They were very attentive.

ROBERT: Yes. (*Pause.*) They were acute.

JOHN: Mmm.

ROBERT: Yes. (*Pause.*) They were discerning.

JOHN: I thought they were.

ROBERT: Perhaps they saw the show tonight (*pause*) on another level. Another, what? another . . . plane, eh? On another level of meaning. Do you know what I mean?

JOHN: I'm not sure I do.

ROBERT: A plane of meaning.

Pause.

JOHN: A plane.

ROBERT: Yes. I feel perhaps they saw a better show than the one we rehearsed.

JOHN: Mmm.

ROBERT: Yes. What are you doing tonight?

JOHN: What am I doing now?

ROBERT: Yes.

JOHN: Going out.

ROBERT: Mmm.

Pause.

JOHN: For dinner.

ROBERT: Yes.

JOHN: I'm famished.

ROBERT: Yes.

JOHN: I haven't had an appetite for several days.

ROBERT: Well, we've opened now.

JOHN: Yes. (*Pause.*) I'm hungry.

ROBERT: Good.

Pause.

JOHN: It almost makes me feel . . .

ROBERT: Go on.

JOHN: As if I'd earned the right . . . (*pause*) I was going to say "to eat," but I'm not sure that that is what I really meant.

ROBERT: What *did* you mean?

JOHN: A show like tonight's show . . .

ROBERT: Yes?

JOHN: Going out there . . .

ROBERT: Yes, go on.

JOHN: It makes me feel fulfilled.

ROBERT: Ah. (*Pause.*) Well, it can do that.

Pause.

JOHN: I liked your scene.

ROBERT: You did.

JOHN: Yes.

ROBERT: Which scene?

JOHN: The courtroom.

ROBERT: You liked that?

JOHN: Yes.

ROBERT: I felt it was off tonight.

JOHN: You didn't.

ROBERT: Yes.

JOHN: It wasn't off to me.

ROBERT: Mmm.

JOHN: It did not seem off to me.

ROBERT: I felt that it was off.

JOHN: If you were off you didn't look it.

ROBERT: No?

JOHN: No.

ROBERT: Mmm.

JOHN: The *doctor* scene . . .

ROBERT: Yes?

JOHN: . . . may have been a trifle . . .

ROBERT: Yes?

JOHN: Well . . .

ROBERT: Say it. What? The doctor scene was what?

    Pause.

JOHN: Brittle.

    Pause.

ROBERT: You thought that it was brittle?

JOHN: Well, I could be wrong.

ROBERT: I trust your judgment.

JOHN: No, I could be wrong. I have been out-of-sorts . . . my eating habits haven't been . . . they've been a little . . .

ROBERT: And you found it brittle, eh?

JOHN: Perhaps. I may have found it so. A bit.

ROBERT: *Overly* brittle?

JOHN: No, not necessarily.

   Pause.

ROBERT: The whole scene?

JOHN: No, no. No. Not the whole scene, no.

ROBERT: What then?

JOHN: A part. A part of it, perhaps.

ROBERT: I wish that you would tell me if you found the whole scene so.

JOHN: It's only an opinion (of a portion of the scene)* and, in the last analysis, we're talking about a *word* . . .

   Pause.

ROBERT: Yes.

JOHN: I'm sorry if I sounded . . .

ROBERT: Not at all. I value your opinion.

JOHN: Yes. I know you do.

ROBERT: Young people in the theatre . . . tomorrow's leaders . . .

   Pause.

JOHN: Yes.

ROBERT: Both of us, or was it only me?

JOHN: Of course not. I told you that I thought *you* were superb. (*Pause.*) *She* was off.

ROBERT: You felt that too, eh?

* Some portions of the dialogue appear in parentheses, which serve to mark a slight change of outlook on the part of the speaker—perhaps a momentary change to a more introspective regard.—D. M.

JOHN: How could I not?

ROBERT: I know. You felt that, eh?

JOHN: I did.

ROBERT: Specifically tonight.

JOHN: Perhaps tonight especially.

ROBERT: Yes. (*Pause.*) Especially tonight.

JOHN: Yes.

ROBERT: Interesting. (*Pause.*) Yes.

JOHN: To me it's a marvel you can work with her at all. (*Pause.*) But to work with her so *well* . . .

ROBERT: You do the best you can.

JOHN: It's enviable.

ROBERT: The show goes on.

JOHN: I find much in that I must admire.

ROBERT: Well, thank you.

JOHN: Not at all.

    Pause.

ROBERT: You have a job to do. You do it by your lights, you bring your expertise to bear, your sense of rightness . . . fellow feelings . . . etiquette . . . professional procedure . . . there are tools one brings to bear . . . procedure.

JOHN: No, it's quite inspiring.

ROBERT: Thank you. (*Pause.*) The mugging is what gets me, eh?

JOHN: Mmm.

ROBERT: Stilted diction and the pregnant pauses I can live with.

JOHN: Yes.

ROBERT: The indicating and the mincing, these are fine, I can accept them.

JOHN: Yes.

ROBERT: But the mugging . . .

JOHN: Yes.

ROBERT: It rots my heart to look at it.

JOHN: I know.

ROBERT: No soul . . . no humanism.

JOHN: No.

ROBERT: No fellow-feeling.

JOHN: No.

ROBERT: I want to kill the cunt.

JOHN: Don't let it worry you.

ROBERT: It doesn't worry me. It just offends my sense of fitness.

JOHN: Mmm.

ROBERT: If I could do her in and be assured I'd get away with it, I'd do it with a clear and open heart.

Pause.

JOHN: Mmm.

ROBERT: That she should be allowed to live (not just to *live* . . . but to parade around a stage . . .)

JOHN: Yes.

ROBERT: And be *paid* for it . . .

JOHN: I totally agree with you.

ROBERT: She would make *anyone* look brittle.

JOHN: Mmm.

ROBERT: You bring me the man capable of looking flexible the moment that she (or those of her ilk) walk on stage.

JOHN: I can't.

ROBERT: No formal training.

JOHN: No.

ROBERT: No sense of right and wrong.

JOHN: She exploits the theatre.

ROBERT: She does.

JOHN: She capitalizes on her beauty.

Pause.

ROBERT: What beauty?

JOHN: Her attractiveness.

ROBERT: Yes.

JOHN: It isn't really beauty.

ROBERT: No.

JOHN: Beauty comes from within.

ROBERT: Yes, I feel it does.

JOHN: She trades on it.

ROBERT: She'll find out. (*Pause.*) Perhaps.

JOHN: It is a marvel you can work with her.

ROBERT: It's not a marvel, John, you learn. You learn control. (*Pause.*) Character. A sense of right from wrong.

JOHN: Yes.

Pause.

ROBERT: I tune her out.

JOHN: Mmm.

ROBERT: When we're on stage, she isn't there for me.

JOHN: Mmmm.

Pause.

ROBERT: How'd you like the table scene?

JOHN: I loved it.

ROBERT: My, that scene was *fun* tonight.

JOHN: It looked it.

ROBERT: Oh, it was.

JOHN: I wanted to be up there with you.

ROBERT: *Did* you?

JOHN: Yes.

ROBERT: Where?

JOHN: Up there.

ROBERT: At the dinner table? (*Pause.*) You mean up there around the dinner table, or up upon the stage?

Pause.

JOHN: In the house.

ROBERT: Around the dinner table?

JOHN: Yes.

ROBERT: Oh, yes, that scene was heaven. (*Pause.*) It made me glad to be alive.

JOHN: It showed.

ROBERT: The *audience* . . .

JOHN: Yes.

ROBERT: That scene was a little play. It was a *poem* tonight.

JOHN: Yes.

ROBERT: Just like a little *walnut*.

JOHN: Yes. (How do you mean?)

ROBERT: *You* know . . .

JOHN: No.

   Pause.

ROBERT: Well, I mean that it was *meaty* . . .

JOHN: Yes . . .

ROBERT: Uh, meaty on the *inside* . . .

JOHN: Yes?

ROBERT: And tight all round.

JOHN: Ah.

   Pause.

ROBERT: Now *that* is superior theatre.

JOHN: Yes. (*Pause.*) Mmm-hmm.

ROBERT: Where did you say you were off to?

JOHN: Now?

ROBERT: Yes.

JOHN: I was going for dinner.

ROBERT: Ah.

JOHN: I've been feeling like a lobster.

ROBERT: Ah.

JOHN: All day.

ROBERT: Mmm. Shellfish.

JOHN: Yes.

   Pause.

ROBERT: I can't eat at night.

JOHN: No.

ROBERT: No. My weight.

JOHN: You're having trouble with your weight?

ROBERT: Yes, always. It's a constant fight.

JOHN: But you're trim enough.

ROBERT: Do you think so?

JOHN: Yes.

ROBERT: Then that makes it worthwhile. (*Pause.*) Thank you.

JOHN: Not at all. What are you up to this evening?

ROBERT: Now, you mean?

JOHN: Yes.

ROBERT: I thought I might go home and read.

JOHN: Ah.

ROBERT: Perhaps take a walk.

JOHN: Ah.

    Pause.

ROBERT: Why'd you ask?

JOHN: No real reason.

ROBERT: Oh.

JOHN: Just asked. I'm just asking.

ROBERT: Well, *I* thought that I'd take a walk.

JOHN: Mmm.

ROBERT: Why did you ask me that?

JOHN: No real reason at all. (*Pause.*) Unless you'd like to join me for a snack?

ROBERT: A "snack." I really couldn't *eat* . . .

Pause.

JOHN: Well, then, some coffee. I could use the company.

ROBERT: I'll walk with you a ways, then.

JOHN: All right.

ROBERT: Good.

Pause.

JOHN: You have some makeup on your face.

ROBERT: Where?

JOHN: There. Behind your ear.

ROBERT: Yes?

JOHN: Here. I'll get it. I'll get you some tissue.

ROBERT: It's all right.

JOHN: No. Wait. We'll get it off.

JOHN *goes after tissue;* ROBERT *stands on the stage.* HE *does vocal exercises.*

ROBERT: Did I get it on my coat?

JOHN: No. (HE *moistens tissue with his saliva and rubs it on* ROBERT's *face.*) There.

ROBERT: Did we get it off?

JOHN: Yes.

ROBERT: Good. I didn't get it on my coat?

JOHN: No.

ROBERT: Good. Good. Thank you.

JOHN: Not at all.

Pause.

ROBERT: Shall we go?

JOHN: Yes.

> JOHN *casually tosses the crumpled tissue toward the trash receptacle Stage Right. It misses the container and falls on the floor.*

ROBERT: Mmm. One moment.

> ROBERT *crosses right, picks up the tissue, and deposits it in the appropriate receptacle.* All right. All gone. Let's go. (*Pause.*) Eh?

JOHN: Yes.

ROBERT: I'm famished.

JOHN: Me too.

ROBERT: Good.

> THEY *exit.*

Scene 2

ROBERT *and* JOHN *in the Wardrobe area.*

ROBERT: Your hat.

    Pause.

JOHN: Thank you.

ROBERT: Like an oven in here.

JOHN: Yes.

ROBERT: Got no space to *breathe.*

JOHN: No. (*Pause.*) Am I in your way?

ROBERT: No. Not at all. (*Pause.*) Quite the contrary.

JOHN (*handing* ROBERT *his hat*): Your hat.

ROBERT: I thank you. (*Pause.*) (*Soliloquizing*) My hat, my hat, my hat. (*Pause.*) Eh?

JOHN: *Mmm.*

Scene 3

Onstage. JOHN *and* ROBERT *in the trenches, smoking the last fag.*

JOHN: They left him up there on the wire.

ROBERT: Calm down.

JOHN: Those bastards.

ROBERT: Yeah.

JOHN: My God. They stuck him on the wire and left him there for target practice.

ROBERT (*of cigarette*): Gimme that.

JOHN: Those dirty, dirty bastards.

ROBERT: Yeah.

JOHN: My God.

ROBERT: Calm down.

JOHN: *He* had a home; *he* had a family. (*Pause.*) Just like them. *He* thought that he was going home. . . .

ROBERT: Relax, we'll all be going home.

JOHN: On the last day, Johnnie, on the *last day* . . .

ROBERT: That's the breaks, kid.

JOHN: Oh, my God, they're signin' it at noon. (*Pause.*) Poor Mahoney. Goes to raise the lousy flag, the Jerries cut him down like wheat . . . Johnnie, two more hours and we're going home. (*Pause.*) And those bastards went and cut him down.

Pause.

ROBERT: That's the breaks.

JOHN: No. Not by me. Uh-*uh.* Not by a long shot.

ROBERT: What are you doing?

JOHN *gets up and peers over the trench.*

What are you doing, Billy?

JOHN *starts over the top.*

JOHN: You hear me, Heinies? Huh? This is for Richard J. Mahoney, Corporal A.E.F., from Dawson, Oklahoma. (*Pause.*) Do you hear me? It's not over yet. Not by a *long* shot. Do you hear me, Huns?

JOHN *runs off right. A single shot is heard, then silence.* ROBERT *draws on his fag deeply, then stubs it out.* HE *uncocks his rifle.*

ROBERT: Well, looks like that's the end of it. . . .

Scene 4

ROBERT *and* JOHN *have just completed a curtain call for an Elizabethan piece.*

ROBERT: Say, keep your point up, will you?

JOHN: When?

ROBERT: When we're down left, eh, right before the head cut. You've been getting lower every night.

JOHN: I'm sorry.

ROBERT: That's all right. Just make sure that you're never in line with my face. I'll show you: Look:

ROBERT *begins to demonstrate the fencing combination.*

You *parry . . . parry . . . THRUST,* but, see, you're thrusting high . . . aaaand *head cut.*

May we try it one more time?

JOHN *nods.*

ROBERT: Good.

THEY *strike a pose and prepare to engage.* THEY *mime the routine as* ROBERT *speaks lines.*

And: "But *fly* my *liege* and *think* no *more* of *me.*" Aaaaand *head cut.*

Eh? You're never in line with my face. We don't want any blood upon the stage.

ROBERT *knocks wood*.

JOHN: No.

Pause.

ROBERT: Please knock on wood.

Pause.

JOHN *knocks*.

Good. Thank you.

Scene 5

ROBERT *and* JOHN *are in a Dance Room.* JOHN *is lounging, sweaty, after working out a bit.* ROBERT *is working at the barre.*

ROBERT: Isn't it strange . . .

JOHN: Yes?

ROBERT: That people will spend time and money on their face and body . . .

JOHN: Mmm?

ROBERT: On smells, textures and appearances . . .

JOHN: Uh huh.

ROBERT: And yet are content to sound like shopgirls and sheepherders.

JOHN: Ummm.

Pause.

ROBERT: It's quite as important as physical beauty.

JOHN: On the stage, you mean.

ROBERT: On the stage and otherwise.

JOHN: Mmm.

ROBERT: *Sound.*

JOHN: Yes.

ROBERT: The crown prince of phenomena.

JOHN: Quite.

ROBERT: An ugly sound, to me, is more offensive than an ugly
odor.

JOHN: Really?

ROBERT: Yes. To me, an ugly *sound* is an extension of an ugly
soul. An indice of lacking aesthetic. (*Pause.*) I don't like
them. I don't like ugly sounds. I don't like the folks that
make them. (*Pause.*) You think that's harsh, don't you?

JOHN: Not at all.

ROBERT: You don't?

JOHN: No.

ROBERT: I know. I'm strange about this. It's a peeve of mine. To
me it's like an odor. Sound. For it emanates from within.
(*Pause.*) Sound and odor germinate within, and are *per-
ceived* within. (*Pause.*) You see?

JOHN: No.

Pause.

ROBERT: All that I am saying is that it comes from within.
(*Pause.*) Sound comes from within. You see?

JOHN: Mmmm.

ROBERT: I am not opposed to odors. (*Pause.*) On principle.

JOHN: No.

Pause.

ROBERT: Do you know when I was young my voice was very
raspy.

JOHN: No.

ROBERT: But I was vain, I was untaught. I felt my vocal quality
—a defect, in effect—was a positive attribute, a contrib-
utory portion of my style.

A LIFE IN THE THEATRE · 23

JOHN: Mmm.

ROBERT: What is style?

JOHN: What?

ROBERT: Style is *nothing*.

JOHN: No?

ROBERT: Style is a paper bag. Its only shape comes from its contents. (*Pause.*) However, I was young. I made a fetish of my imperfections.

JOHN: It's a common fault.

ROBERT: It makes me blush today to think about it.

Pause.

JOHN: Don't think about it.

Pause.

ROBERT: You're right. You start from the beginning and go through the middle and wind up at the end.

JOHN: Yes.

Pause.

ROBERT: A little like a play. Keep your back straight.

JOHN: Mmm.

ROBERT: We must not be afraid of process.

JOHN: No.

ROBERT: We must not lie about our antecedents.

JOHN: No.

ROBERT: We must not be second-class citizens. (*Pause.*) We must not be clowns whose sole desire is to please. We have a right to learn.

Pause.

JOHN: Is my back straight?

ROBERT: No. (*Pause.*) Do you *follow* me?

JOHN: I think I do.

ROBERT: We must not be afraid to *grow*. We must support each other, John. This is the wondrous thing *about* the theatre, this potential.

JOHN: Mmmm.

ROBERT: Our history goes back as far as Man's. Our aspirations in the Theatre are much the *same* as man's. (*Pause.*) (Don't you think?)

JOHN: Yes.

Pause.

ROBERT: We *are* society. Keep your back straight, John. The mirror is your friend. (*Pause.*) For a few more years. (*Pause.*) What have we to fear, John, from *phenomena?* (*Pause.*) We are explorers of the *soul.*

Pause.

JOHN: Is my back straight?

ROBERT: No.

Scene 6

The end of a day. JOHN *is on the backstage telephone.*

JOHN: Oh, no. I can't. I'm going out with someone in the show. (*Pause.*) No, in fact, an *Actor*. (*Pause.*) I don't know . . . Midnight. (*Pause.*) I'd like that very much. (*Pause.*) Me, too. (*Pause.*) How have you been?

ROBERT *enters.*

ROBERT: You ready?

JOHN (*covering phone*): Yes. (*into phone*) I'll see you then. (*Pause.*) 'Bye.

HE *hangs up telephone.*

ROBERT: We all must have an outside life, John. This is an essential.

JOHN: Yes.

ROBERT: Who was it?

Pause.

JOHN: A friend.

Scene 7

A short scene in which JOHN *and* ROBERT *encounter each other coming into the theatre for an early-morning rehearsal.*

ROBERT: Good morning.

JOHN: Morning.

ROBERT: 'Nother day, eh?

JOHN: Yes.

ROBERT: Another day. (HE *sighs.*) Another day.

Scene 8

Before a performance—at the makeup table.

JOHN: May I have the tissue, please? Thank you. How do you feel this evening?

ROBERT: Tight. I feel a little tight. It's going to be a vibrant show tonight. I feel coiled up.

JOHN: Mmm.

ROBERT: But I don't feel tense.

JOHN: No?

ROBERT: No. Never feel tense. I almost never feel tense on stage. I feel ready to act. That's a lovely brush.

JOHN: This?

ROBERT: No. The quarter-inch.

JOHN: This one?

ROBERT: Yes. Is it new?

JOHN: It's an eighth-inch.

ROBERT: That one?

JOHN: Yes.

ROBERT: That's an eighth-inch?

JOHN: Yes.

Pause.

ROBERT: Well, it's awfully splayed, don't you think?

JOHN: No.

ROBERT: It's not splayed a bit?

JOHN: No.

ROBERT: Well, it's not *new* . . . (Is it new?)

JOHN: No, I've had it a while.

ROBERT: A while, eh?

JOHN: Yes.

ROBERT: A long while?

JOHN: Yes.

ROBERT: What is it, camel?

JOHN: It's sable.

> *Pause.*

ROBERT: (Sable brushes.) You keep your things well.

JOHN: Mmm.

ROBERT: It's impressive. No. It's one of the things which impressed me first about you.

JOHN: Mmm.

ROBERT: You take excellent care of your tools. (*Pause.*) May I ask you something, John?

JOHN: Of course.

ROBERT: Could you do me a favor?

JOHN: What?

> *Pause.*

ROBERT: In our scene tonight . . .

JOHN: Yes?

ROBERT: Mmmm . . .

JOHN: What?

ROBERT: Could you . . . perhaps . . . *do* less?

JOHN: *Do* less?

ROBERT: Yes.

JOHN: *Do* less???

ROBERT: Yes . . .

> *Pause.*

JOHN: Do less *what???*

ROBERT: You know.

JOHN: You mean . . . what do you mean?

> *Pause.*

ROBERT: You know.

JOHN: Do you mean I'm walking on your scene? (*Pause.*) What do you mean?

ROBERT: Nothing. It's a thought I had. An aesthetic consideration.

JOHN: Mmm.

ROBERT: I thought maybe if you *did* less . . .

JOHN: Yes?

ROBERT: *You* know.

JOHN: If I *did* less.

ROBERT: Yes.

JOHN: Well, thank you for the thought.

ROBERT: I don't think you have to be like that.

JOHN: I'm sorry.

ROBERT: Are you?

JOHN: I accept the comment in the spirit in which it was, I am sure, intended.

   Pause.

ROBERT: It *was* intended in that spirit, John.

JOHN: I know it was.

ROBERT: How could it be intended otherwise?

JOHN: It couldn't.

ROBERT: Well, you *know* it couldn't.

JOHN: Yes, I know.

ROBERT: It hurts me when you take it personally. (HE *stands.*) Shit!

JOHN: What?

ROBERT: My zipper's broken.

JOHN: Do you want a safety pin?

ROBERT: I have one.

JOHN (*rising, starting to leave*): Do you want me to send the woman in?

ROBERT: No. No. I'll manage. Shit. Oh, shit.

JOHN: You're sure?

ROBERT: Yes.

JOHN: You don't want the woman?

ROBERT: No. I do not want the woman. Thank you.

JOHN: You want me to pin it for you?

ROBERT: No.

JOHN: I'll do it. Let me pin it for you.

ROBERT: No. Thank you. No. I'll get it.

JOHN: Oh, come on. I'll do it. Come on.

> JOHN *pulls out chair.*

Get up here. Come on. Get up.

> ROBERT *gets up on the chair.* Give me the pin. Come on.

> ROBERT *hands* JOHN *the pin.* JOHN *drops it on the floor.*
> Shit.

> JOHN *gets down on hands and knees to look for it.*

ROBERT: Oh, Christ.

JOHN: You got another one?

ROBERT: No. Oh, Christ, come on. Come on.

JOHN: I'm *looking* for it, for God's sake.

ROBERT: There!

JOHN: Stand still now.

ROBERT: Come on, come on.

> JOHN *attempts to pin* ROBERT'S *fly.*

Put it in.

JOHN: Just hold still for a moment.

ROBERT: Come *on,* for God's sake!

JOHN: All right. All right. You know, I think you're gaining
weight . . .

ROBERT: Oh, fuck you. Will you stick it in?

JOHN: Hold still. There.

ROBERT: Thanks a lot.

> HE *gets off the chair.*

JOHN: Good show!

ROBERT: Thank you.

Scene 9

Onstage. A scene from a play in a lawyer's office. ROBERT *is behind a desk, talking on the telephone.*

ROBERT: Perhaps you find it harsh, but I do not. I've always felt that we were friends. (*Pause.*) I know you have, and so have I.

JOHN enters the office. ROBERT motions him to sit.

I know you have. I feel that there is some common ground, I feel our interests are similar. (*Pause.*) No, not identical, but similar, certainly negotiable.

ROBERT offers JOHN a cigar from a humidor. JOHN refuses.

(*Pause.*) I've always felt so. (*Pause.*) When? (*Pause.*) I'm sorry, I'm tied up the entire morning. (*Pause.*) Yes? (*Pause.*) Yes?

JOHN rises and walks over to look out the window.

All right, then. (*Pause.*) And I'm sure this can be settled to our mutual satisfaction. (*Pause.*) So do I. I'll have my girl take care of it. (*Pause.*) Not at all. (*Pause.*) Not at all. (*Pause.*) And the very same to you. (*Pause.*) Good-bye.

(HE *hangs up the telephone. To* JOHN): Forgive me, David.

JOHN: Not at all. I've just been admiring the view.

ROBERT: Lovely, isn't it?

JOHN: I should think one would get used to it.

ROBERT: Well, it's been thirteen years, and I haven't seemed to do so.

JOHN: Yes. (*Pause.*) It's funny, you know, how things attain the force of habit . . .

ROBERT: The force of habit . . . yes.

JOHN: Take me and Gillian.

Pause.

ROBERT: Yes? (*Pause.*) Is that what you've come to talk about?

(*The intercom rings.* ROBERT *into intercom*) Hold all calls, please. (*To* JOHN) Is there something wrong between you and Gillian?

JOHN: Gillian's going to have a baby.

ROBERT: Why, this is marvelous. How long have you known?

JOHN: Since this morning.

ROBERT: How marvelous!

JOHN: It isn't mine.

ROBERT: It's not.

JOHN: No.

ROBERT: Oh. (*Pause.*) I always supposed there was something one *said* in these situations . . . but I find . . . Do you know—that is, have you been told who the father is?

JOHN: Yes.

ROBERT: Really. Who is it, David?

JOHN: It's you, John.

ROBERT: Me!

JOHN: You.

ROBERT: No.

JOHN: Yes.

ROBERT: How preposterous.

JOHN: Is it?

ROBERT: You know it is.

JOHN: Do I?

ROBERT: Yes.

JOHN: Oh, John, John, John. (*Pause.*) I think that I'll have that cigar now.

ROBERT: I think that I'll join you. (*Pause.*) She's told you that I am the husband.

Pause.

JOHN: No.

Pause.

ROBERT: She's told you that I am the father.

JOHN: Yes. (*Pause.*) What are we going to do about this?

ROBERT: I don't know, David. You could—I suppose you could do me some physical damage. . . .

JOHN: Yes.

ROBERT: Or we could sit and discuss this as gentlemen. Which would you prefer?

JOHN: Which, in the end, is more civilized, John?

ROBERT: I don't know, David, I don't know. (*Long pause . . . intercom rings*) I asked you to hold all calls. (*Pause.*) Perhaps *you* should take this.

Scene 10

Backstage in the Wardrobe area.

ROBERT: The motherfucking leeches. The sots. (*Pause.*) The bloody boors. All of them . . . All of them . . .

JOHN: Who?

ROBERT: All of them.

JOHN: All of whom?

Pause.

ROBERT: What?

JOHN: All of whom?

Pause.

ROBERT: You know. All of them. Bloody shits . . .

JOHN: What about them?

ROBERT: Why can they not leave us alone? (*Pause.*) Eh?

JOHN: Yes.

ROBERT: What? Eh?

JOHN: Yes.

ROBERT: You're damn right. (*Sotto voce*) Boring lunatics . . .

Scene 11

Onstage.

JOHN: Oh, the autumn.

Pause.

ROBERT: Yes.

JOHN: Autumn weather.

ROBERT: Yes.

JOHN: Oh, for the sun.

ROBERT: Will you pass me my robe, please?

JOHN: Your laprobe.

ROBERT: Yes. (*Business.*)

JOHN: Maman says just one more day, one more day, yet another week.

ROBERT: Mmm.

JOHN: One more week.

ROBERT: Would you please close the window?

JOHN: What? I'm sorry?

ROBERT: Do you feel a draft?

JOHN: A slight draft, yes. (*Pause.*) Shall I close the window?

ROBERT: Would you mind?

JOHN: No, not at all. (I love this window.) (*Pause.*) (*Closes the window.*)

ROBERT: Thank you.

JOHN: Mmm.

ROBERT: This room . . . this room.

JOHN: If we could leave this afternoon.

ROBERT: Mmm?

JOHN: If we could just call . . . bring the carriage round, just leave this afternoon . . .

ROBERT: It's much too cold . . .

JOHN: Just throw two shirts into a bag . . . a scarf . . .

ROBERT: (. . . the roads . . .)

JOHN: Just meet the train. (*Pause.*) Venice . . .

Pause.

ROBERT: It's much too cold.

Pause.

JOHN: Would you like a glass of tea?

ROBERT: What? Thank you, yes.

JOHN: I like this room.

ROBERT: Yes, so do I.

JOHN: I always have.

Pause.

ROBERT: So have I.

JOHN: I'll ring for tea.

Pause.

ROBERT: Thank you.

Scene 12

Backstage. ROBERT *and* JOHN *changing clothes.*

ROBERT: I wish they'd wash this stuff more often.

JOHN: Mmm.

ROBERT: Smells like a gym in here.

JOHN: The building's old.

ROBERT: Yes. Yes. (*Pause.*) Tired?

JOHN: No. A little.

ROBERT: Mmm.

Scene 13

JOHN *and* ROBERT *are sitting and reading a new script.*

ROBERT: Good. All right. Got a match?

JOHN *lights* ROBERT'*s cigarette.*

Mmm. Thank you.

JOHN: Mmm.

ROBERT: All right. Good. (*Starts reading*) "One day blends into the next" . . . I'm not going to do the accent. Eh?

JOHN: Yes.

ROBERT: Good. One day blends into the next. Scorching sun . . . shiv'ring moon. Salt . . . saltwater. . . .

JOHN: "It'll rain soon" . . .   ROBERT (*musing*): Salt . . . I'm sorry?   saltwater . . .

ROBERT: Eh?

JOHN: I'm sorry. What?

ROBERT: No, I'm just thinking. Salt. Saltwater. Eh? The thought. He lets you see the thought there.

Pause.

JOHN: Mmm.

Pause.

ROBERT: Salt! Sweat. His life flows out. (*Pause.*) Then salt*water!* Eh?

JOHN: Yes.

ROBERT: To the *sea*.

JOHN: Yes.

ROBERT: All right. Good.

> THEY *go back.*

> "One day blends into the next. Salt. Saltwater."

JOHN: "It'll rain soon."

ROBERT: "Rain? What do *you* know about it?" (*Pause.*) "I've spent my whole life on the sea, and all that I know is the length of my ignorance. Which is *complete,* sonny." (*Pause.*) "My ignorance is complete."

JOHN: "It's gotta rain."

ROBERT: The motif, eh, the leitmotif. He takes the descant through the scene—"It's got to rain." You look at it, he does the same thing through the play.

> *Pause.*

JOHN: Mmm.

ROBERT: Go on.

> *Pause.*

JOHN: "It's gotta rain."

ROBERT: "Tell it to the marines."

JOHN: "It doesn't rain, I'm going off my nut."

ROBERT: You see: it *will* rain, it's *got* to rain, it *doesn't* rain. . . . all right, all right. "Just take it easy, kid . . . what you don't want to do now is sweat." (*Pause.*) "Believe me."

> *Pause.*

JOHN: "We're never getting out of this alive." (*Pause.*) "Are we?"

ROBERT: "How do you want it?"

JOHN: "Give it to me straight."

Pause.

ROBERT: "Kid, we haven't got a chance in hell." (*Pause. Musing*) "We haven't got a chance in hell. We're never getting out of this alive." (*Pause.*) Eh? He sets it on the sea, we are marooned, he tells us that the sea is life, and then we're never getting out of it alive. (*Pause.*) Eh?

Pause.

JOHN: Yes.

ROBERT: The man could write . . . All right. All right. (*Pause.*) Let's go back a bit.

Pause.

JOHN (*sighs*): "It'll rain soon . . ."

Scene 14

ROBERT *and* JOHN *are eating Chinese food at the makeup table between shows.*

ROBERT: You had an audition this afternoon, eh?

JOHN: Yes.

ROBERT: How did it go?

JOHN: Well, I thought.

ROBERT: Yes?

Pause.

JOHN: They were receptive. I thought it went well.

ROBERT: How did you feel?

JOHN: I felt good; they liked it.

ROBERT: That's nice.

JOHN: I thought so.

ROBERT: That's very nice. (*Pause. Eating*) There are two classes of phenomena.

JOHN: There are.

Pause.

ROBERT: There are those things we *can* control and those things which we cannot.

JOHN: Mmm.

ROBERT: You can't control what someone thinks of you.

JOHN: No.

ROBERT: That is up to them. They may be glum, they may be out-of-sorts. Perhaps they are neurotic.

JOHN: How's your duck?

ROBERT: Fine. (*Pause.*) One *can* control, however, one's actions. One's intentions.

JOHN: Pass the bread, please.

ROBERT: That is all one can control.

JOHN: Please pass the bread.

ROBERT: You're eating bread?

JOHN: Yes.

ROBERT: Oh. (*Pause.*) Here it is.

JOHN: Thanks.

ROBERT: If they hadn't liked you, that would not have signified that you weren't a good actor.

JOHN: No. I think I know that.

ROBERT: Yes. I think perhaps you do. (*Pause.*) Yes. I'm glad they liked you, though.

JOHN: Thank you.

ROBERT: You think they're going to hire you?

JOHN: I don't know.

ROBERT: Well, I hope they do.

JOHN: I hope so, too.

ROBERT: That would be nice for you.

JOHN: Yes.

    Pause.

ROBERT (*to self*): Good things for good folk.

Scene 15

JOHN *and* ROBERT *are dressing backstage.*

ROBERT: We should do this whole frigging thing in rehearsal clothes, you know? Eh? Do it in blue jeans and T-shirts and give it some life, you know?

JOHN: Yes.

ROBERT: Eh? And give it some *guts.* (*Pause.*) Give *guts* to it. (*Pause.*) And to hell with experimentation. Artistic experimentation is shit. Huh?

JOHN: Right.

ROBERT: You're frigging well told. (*Pause.*) Two *actors,* some *lines* . . . and an audience. That's what I say. Fuck 'em all.

Scene 16

Onstage. The Barricades.

ROBERT: And the people cry for truth; the people cry for freedom from the vicious lies and slanders of the ages . . . the slanders of the body and the soul. The heart cries out: the memory says man has always lived in chains . . . has always lived in chains . . . (*Pause.*) Bread, bread, bread, the people scream . . . we drown their screaming with our heads in cups, in books . . . in newspapers . . . between the breasts of women . . . in our work . . . enough. A new day rises . . . those who must connect themselves to yesterday for succor will be left behind . . . their souls are in the histories, their heads on pikes around the buildings of our government. Now we must look ahead. . . . Our heads between the breasts of women, plight our troth to that security far greater than protection of mere rank or fortune. Now: we must dedicate ourselves to spirit: to the spirit of humanity; to life. (*Pause.*) To the barricades! (*Pause.*) Bread, bread, bread.

Scene 17

At the makeup table.

ROBERT: A makeup table. Artificial light. The scent of powder. Tools. Sticks. Brushes. Tissues. (*Pause.*) Cold *cream.* (*Pause.*) Greasepaint. (*Pause.*) Greasepaint! What is it? Some cream base, some coloring . . . texture, smell, color . . . analyze it and what have you? Meaningless component parts, though one could likely say the same for anything. . . . *But* mix and package it, affix a label, set it on a makeup table . . . a brush or two . . .

JOHN: Would you please shut up?

Pause.

ROBERT: Am I disturbing you?

JOHN: You are.

Pause.

ROBERT: Enough to justify this breach of etiquette?

JOHN: What breach? What etiquette?

ROBERT: John . . .

JOHN: Yes?

ROBERT: When one's been in the theatre as long as I . . .

JOHN: Can we do this later?

ROBERT: I feel that there is something here of worth to you.

JOHN: You do?

ROBERT: Yes.

JOHN (*sighs*): Let us hear it then.

ROBERT: All right. You know your attitude, John, is not of the best. It isn't. It just isn't.

JOHN (*Pause*): It isn't?

ROBERT: Forms. The Theatre's a closed society. Constantly abutting thoughts, the feelings, the emotions of our colleagues. Sensibilities (*pause*) bodies . . . *forms* evolve. An etiquette, eh? In our personal relations with each other. Eh, John? In our personal relationships.

Pause.

JOHN: Mmm.

ROBERT: One generation sows the seeds. It instructs the preceding . . . that is to say, the *following* generation . . . from the quality of its actions. Not from its discourse, John, no, but organically. (*Pause.*) You can learn a lot from keeping your mouth shut.

JOHN: You can.

ROBERT: Yes. And perhaps this is not the place to speak of attitudes.

JOHN: Before we go on.

ROBERT: Yes. But what is "life on stage" but attitudes?

JOHN (*Pause*): What?

ROBERT: Damn little.

Pause.

JOHN: May I use your brush?

ROBERT: Yes. (*Hands* JOHN *brush.*) One must speak of these things, John, or we will go the way of all society.

JOHN: Which is what?

ROBERT: Take too much for granted, fall away and die. (*Pause.*) On the boards, or in society at large. There must be law, there must be a reason, there must be tradition.

Pause.

JOHN: I'm sorry that I told you to shut up.

ROBERT: No, you can't buy me off that cheaply.

JOHN: No?

ROBERT: No.

Pause.

JOHN: Would you pass me the cream, please?

ROBERT: Certainly. (*Passes the cream.*) Here is the cream.

JOHN: Thank you.

ROBERT: Wait. I know what the line is. . . .

JOHN: What?

ROBERT: Uh, after you give her the watch, right?

JOHN: Yes.

ROBERT: Right. You give her the *watch*. You give her the *watch* . . .

JOHN: And?

ROBERT: Ah, Christ . . . you hand the cunt the watch: "Ma'am, we kinda thought that maybe . . ."

JOHN: "The men all got together, ma'am . . ."

ROBERT: Yes. And . . . um . . . this is ridiculous . . . You give her the *watch* . . . (What's *her* line?)

JOHN: "Thank you."

Pause.

ROBERT: Ah, fuck. You'd better get a script. You want me to?

JOHN: Sshhhhh!

Pause.

ROBERT: What?

JOHN: Shut up. I'm trying to hear my cue.

Pause.

ROBERT: What's happening?

Pause.

JOHN: I think I missed my cue. (*Pause.*) I think I missed my cue.

Pause.

ROBERT: What's happening?

JOHN: Sshhhhhhh!

Scene 18

Onstage. The famous lifeboat scene.

ROBERT: One day blends into the next. Scorching sun, shivering moon. Salt. Saltwater . . .

JOHN: It'll rain soon.

ROBERT: Rain . . . ? What do *you* know about it? (*Pause.*) I've spent my whole life on the sea, and all that I know is the length of my ignorance. Which is *complete,* sonny. (*Pause.*) My ignorance is complete.

JOHN: It's gotta rain.

ROBERT: Tell it to the marines.

JOHN: It doesn't rain, I'm going off my nut.

ROBERT: Just take it easy, kid. . . . What you don't wanna do now is sweat. (*Pause.*) Believe me.

Pause.

JOHN: We're never getting out of this alive. (*Pause.*) Are we?

ROBERT: How do you want it?

JOHN: Give it to me straight.

ROBERT: Kid, we haven't got a chance in hell. (*Pause.*) But you know what? (*Pause.*) You shouldn't let it get you down. And you know why? 'Cause that's the gamble. That's what life on the sea is about.

JOHN: Can I tell you something?

ROBERT: Shoot.

JOHN: You're full of it, I mean it. Don't you tell me about Men and the Sea, because that's been out of the picture for years. If it ever existed. No, it probably did. Back in the days when a man had a stake in what he went out after, when he had a stake in his ship . . . and a stake in himself. . . . But *now* . . . Now we're dyin' 'cause some black bastard ship-owner in Newport decided that rather than make his ships safe for men, it was cheaper to overinsure them. (*Pause.*) *THAT'S* what we're dying for . . .

Pause. The KID *breaks down.*

ROBERT: Danny . . . Danny . . . A ship! ! ! *A SHIP! ! !*

Scene 19

JOHN *and* ROBERT *are standing in the wings.* JOHN *is about to go on.*

ROBERT: Ephemeris, ephemeris, eh?

JOHN: What?

ROBERT: Ephemeris, ephemeris.

Pause.

JOHN: What are you saying?

ROBERT: Time passes.

Pause.

JOHN: What comes after: "The men got together, ma'am, and we kind of thought you'd like to have this"?

ROBERT: She says, "Thank you."

JOHN: I'm aware of that, I think. *After* that. What comes after that?

ROBERT: Your line?

JOHN: Yes.

ROBERT: Uh . . .

JOHN: Have you got a script?

ROBERT: What would I be doing with a script?

JOHN: I'm going to go get a script.

ROBERT: Can you see?

JOHN: I'm *going* on. (*Pause.*) I'm going to go on. (*Pause*). What do you think?

ROBERT *shrugs. Pause.*

Christ. I'm going out. . . .

ROBERT: You want me to get a script?

JOHN: I've missed my cue. . . . I've missed my cue. . . .

ROBERT: Well, go out there . . . go on.

Pause.

JOHN: Oh, God. I've missed my cue. . . .

ROBERT: Get *out* there. . . .

JOHN (*making his entrance*): "Missus Wilcox??? Missus Wilcox, ma'am? The men all got together. . . ."

Scene 20

Backstage. JOHN *is dressing.* ROBERT *enters, speaking slowly to himself.*

ROBERT: Oh God, oh God, oh God, oh God, oh God. (*He sees* JOHN. *Pause.*) New sweater?

JOHN: Yes.

ROBERT: Nice.

JOHN: Mmm.

ROBERT: What is it?

JOHN: What?

ROBERT: What is it? Cashmere?

JOHN: I don't know.

ROBERT: Looks good on you.

JOHN: Thanks.

ROBERT: Mmm.

Scene 21

Backstage. JOHN *is at the telephone, waiting.* ROBERT *enters.*

ROBERT: And everybody wants a piece. They all have got to get a piece.

JOHN (*into phone*): I'll wait.

ROBERT: We spend our adult lives bending over for incompetents. For ten-percenters, sweetheart unions, everybody in the same bed together. Agents. All the bloodsuckers. The robbers of the cenotaph. Who are we?

JOHN: Who? (*into phone*) Hello?

ROBERT: Who indeed?

JOHN: I'm holding for Miss Erenstein.

ROBERT: If we cannot speak to each other . . . what do we have but our fellow workers? If we do not have that, what do we have? Who can speak our language, eh?

JOHN (*to* ROBERT): And what of talent?

ROBERT: And what of it? (*Pause.*) What of humanity?

   Pause.

JOHN: What?

ROBERT: I don't know. (*Pause.*) Let's get a drink.

JOHN: I'm on the phone.

ROBERT: Hang it up.

JOHN (*into phone*): Hello, Bonnie? *John.* How *are* you . . . ?

ROBERT: We enslave ourselves.

JOHN (*into phone*): *No!*

ROBERT: (God.)

JOHN (*into phone*): Why, *thank* you. Thank you very much. (*Pause.*) On the *film* . . . ? Yes? Yes? I'll check my book.

ROBERT: One does not have to check one's "book" to get a *drink*. (*To himself*) A drink cannot buy *itself*.

JOHN (*covering phone*): Do you know who this *is?*

ROBERT: I am going to drink. For I must drink now. Do you know why?

JOHN: Why?

> *Pause.*

ROBERT: It is fitting. (*Exits.*)

JOHN (*into phone*): Yes. Eleven's *fine*. (*Pause.*) *W*onderful.

Scene 22

Backstage. ROBERT *and* JOHN *are taking off their makeup.*

ROBERT: Fucking leeches.

JOHN: Mmm. Pass me the tissue, please?

ROBERT: They'll praise you for the things you never did and pan you for a split second of godliness. What do they know? They create nothing. They come in the front door. They don't even buy a ticket.

JOHN: No.

ROBERT: They've praised you too much. I do not mean to detract from your reviews—you deserve praise, John, much praise.

JOHN: Thank you.

ROBERT: Not, however, for those things which they have praised you for.

JOHN: In your opinion.

ROBERT: Yes, John, yes. From now on. (*Pause.*) You must be very careful who you listen to. From whom you take advice.

JOHN: Yes.

ROBERT: Never take *advice* . . .

JOHN: Yes . . .

ROBERT: . . . from *people* . . .

JOHN: May I have my comb, please?

ROBERT: . . . who do not have a vested interest, John, in your eventual success.

JOHN: I won't.

ROBERT: Or, barring that, in Beauty in the Theatre.

JOHN: I thought that they were rather to the point.

ROBERT: You did.

JOHN: Yes.

ROBERT: Your reviews.

JOHN: Yes.

ROBERT: All false modesty aside.

JOHN: Yes.

ROBERT: Oh, the Young, the Young, the Young, the Young.

JOHN: The Farmer in the Dell.

ROBERT: Oh, I see.

JOHN: Would you hand me my scarf, please?

    Pause.

ROBERT: You fucking TWIT.

JOHN: I beg your pardon?

ROBERT: I think that you heard me. (*Takes towel from* JOHN'S *area and begins to use it.*)

    Pause.

JOHN: Robert.

ROBERT: What?

JOHN: Use your own towels from now on.

ROBERT: They're at the laundry.

JOHN: Get them back.

Scene 23

A dark stage, one worklight lit. JOHN *is rehearsing.*

JOHN: Now all the youth of England are on fire
And silken dalliance in the wardrobe lies.
Now thrive the Armourers and honor's thought
Reigns solely in the breast of every man.

ROBERT (*offstage*): Ah, sweet poison of the actor, rehearsing in
an empty theatre upon an empty stage . . .

JOHN: Good evening.

ROBERT: . . . but full of life, full of action, full of resolve, full of
youth. (*Pause.*) Please continue. (*Pause.*) Please, please
continue. I'd like you to. . . . I'm sorry. Does this upset
you? Does it upset you that someone is watching? I'm sorry,
I can understand that. (*Pause.*) It's good. It's *quite* good. I
was watching you for a while. I hope you don't mind. Do
you mind?

JOHN: I've only been here a minute or so.

ROBERT: And I've watched you all that time. It seemed so long.
It was so full. You're very good, John. Have I told you that
lately? You are becoming a very fine actor. The flaws of
youth are the perquisite of the young. It is the perquisite of
the young to possess the flaws of youth.

JOHN: It's fitting, yes. . . .

ROBERT: Ah, don't mock me, John. You shouldn't mock me. It's
too easy. It's not good for you, no. And that is a lesson
which we have to learn. (*Pause.*) Which you have to learn.

JOHN: And what is that?

ROBERT: That it is a hurtful fault, John, to confuse sincerity with weakness. (*Pause.*) And I must tell you something.

JOHN: Yes.

ROBERT: About the Theatre—and this is a wondrous thing about the Theatre—and John, one of the ways in which it's most like life . . .

JOHN: And what is that?

Pause.

ROBERT: Simply this. That in the *Theatre* (as in life—and the Theatre is, of course, a *part* of life . . . No?) . . . Do you see what I'm saying? I'm saying, as in a grocery store, that you cannot separate the *time* one spends . . . that is, it's all part of one's *life*. (*Pause.*) In addition to the fact that what's happening on *stage* is life . . . of a sort . . . I mean, it's part of your *life*. (*Pause.*) Which is one reason I'm so *gratified* (if I may presume, and I recognize that it may be a presumption) to see you . . . to see the *young* of the Theatre . . . (And it's *not* unlike one's children) . . . following in the footpaths of . . . following in the footsteps of . . . those who have gone before. (*Pause.*) Do you see what I am saying? I would like to think you *did*. Do you? John? (*Pause.*) Well . . . well. Goodnight, John.

Pause.

JOHN: Goodnight.

ROBERT: *Good*night. I'll see you.

HE *waves, starts to exit.*

JOHN: *Good* night. (*Long pause.*)

JOHN *examines the wings where* ROBERT *has exited.* JOHN *takes the stage.*

They sell the pasture now to buy the horse
Following the mirror of all Christian Kings
With the winged heels as English Mercuries.

Pause.

For now sits Expectation in the air

Pause.

And hides a sword.

Pause. HE *talks into the wings*

Are you back in there? Robert? Are you back in there? (*Pause.*) I *see* you in there. I see you there, Robert.

ROBERT: (*offstage voice*): I'm just leaving.

JOHN: You were not just leaving, you were . . . *looking* at me.

ROBERT: On my way *out,* John. On my way *out.* Christ, but you make me feel small. You make me feel *small,* John. I don't feel good.

Pause.

JOHN: Are you crying? Are you crying, Robert, for chrissakes? (*Pause.*) *Christ.* Are you crying?

ROBERT: Yes.

Pause.

JOHN: Well, stop *crying.*

ROBERT: Yes. I will.

JOHN: No, stop it *now.* Stop it. Please.

Pause. ROBERT *stops crying.*

ROBERT: Better?

Pause.

JOHN: Yes. (*Pause.*) Are you all right?

ROBERT: Oh, yes. I'm all right. I'm fine. Thank you, John. (*Pause.*) Well, I suppose I'll . . . (You're going to work summore, eh?)

JOHN: Yes.

ROBERT: Then I suppose I'll . . . (Well, I was leaving *anyway.*) (*Pause.*) Goodnight. Goodnight, John.

Pause.

JOHN: Are you all right now? (*raising his voice*) Robert! Are you all right now?

ROBERT (*far offstage*): Yes. Thank you. Yes. I'm all right now.

Pause.

JOHN *takes the stage again, is about to begin declaiming.*

ROBERT (*from far offstage*): You're not angry with me, are you?

JOHN: No.

ROBERT: You're sure?

JOHN: Yes.

Pause.

ROBERT: I'm glad, John. (*Pause.*) Thank you.

JOHN: Goodnight, Robert. (*Pause.*) Robert? (*Pause.*)

JOHN *takes the stage.*

Now all the Youth of England are on fire . . .

Pause.

Robert?

Pause.

ROBERT: Yes, John?

JOHN: Are you out there?

ROBERT: Yes, John.

JOHN (*sotto voce*): Shit.

Scene 24

Onstage. ROBERT *and* JOHN *are dressed in surgical smocks, and stand behind a form on an operating table.*

ROBERT: Give me some suction there, doctor, will you . . . that's good.

JOHN: Christ, what I wouldn't give for a cigarette.

ROBERT: Waaal, just a few more minutes and I think I'll join you in one. (*Pause.*) Nervous, Jimmy?

JOHN: No. Yes.

ROBERT: No need to be. A few years, you'll be doing these in your sleep. Suction. Retractor. (*Business.*) No, the *large* retractor.

JOHN: Sorry.

ROBERT: It's all right. Give me another one, will you?

(*Business*)

JOHN (*pointing*): What's that?

Pause. ROBERT *shakes his head minutely.* JOHN *nods his head.*

What's that?

ROBERT *minutely but emphatically shakes his head.*

Pause.

JOHN *mumbles something to* ROBERT. ROBERT *mumbles something to* JOHN.

Pause.

ROBERT: Would you, uh, can you give me some sort of reading on the, uh, electro . . . um . . . on the . . . . Would you get me one, please? (*motioning* JOHN *offstage*) No . . . on the, uh . . . would you get me a reading on this man?

JOHN (*pointing*): What's *that!!!?*

ROBERT: What is what? Eh?

JOHN: What's that near his spleen? (*Pause.*) A curious growth near his spleen?

ROBERT: What?

JOHN: A Curious Growth Near His Spleen? (*Pause.*) Is that one, there?

ROBERT: No, I think not. I think you cannot see a growth near his spleen for some *time* yet. So would you (as this man's in shock) . . . would you get me, please, give me a reading on his vital statements. Uh, *Functions.* . . ? Would you do that one thing for me, please?

JOHN (*sotto voce*): We've done that one, Robert.

ROBERT: I fear I must disagree with you, Doctor. Would you give me a reading on his vital *things,* if you please? Would you? (*Pause.*) For the love of God?

JOHN (*sotto voce*): That's in the other part.

ROBERT: No, it is *not.* He's in shock. He's in shock, and I'm becoming miffed with you. Now: if you desire to work in this business again, will you give me a reading? If you wish to continue here inside the hospital? (*Pause.*) Must I call a *policeman!!?* (*Pause.*) Have you no feeling? This man's in deepest shock!!!

Pause. JOHN *takes off his mask and walks away.*

And now where are you going? (*Pause.*) You *quitter!!*

(Another pause.) *(To audience)*

Ladies and gentlemen. What we have seen here today is—I won't say a *"perfect"*—but a very good example of successful surgical technique, performed under modern optimum conditions, uh . . . and with a minimum of *fuss* . . . a minimum of *mess* and *bother* . . . and I hope that you have . . . *(The curtain is being rung down on him)* . . . that you have found it every bit . . .

Curtain is down. Hold.

ROBERT *(generally)* : Does anybody have a script?

Scene 25

Backstage. ROBERT *appears, holding his left wrist with his right hand.*

ROBERT: Oh God, oh God, I've cut myself.

JOHN (*entering*): What have you done?

ROBERT: I'm bleeding. Oh, my God . . .

JOHN: Christ.

ROBERT: What a silly accident. Can you believe this?

JOHN: Come on.

ROBERT: Where?

JOHN: We're going to the hospital.

ROBERT: Oh, no. Oh, no. I'm all right, really.

JOHN: Come on.

ROBERT: No. What would they say? Kidding aside. (*Pause.*) No. I'm quite all right. My razor slipped and now I'm fine. I had a moment, though. I did. (*Pause.*) John . . . (*Pause.*) John . . .

JOHN: Yes?

ROBERT: Did you know in olden times they used to say "clean-shaven like an actor"? (*Pause.*) Did you know that?

JOHN: Are you all right?

ROBERT: Oh, yes. I'm fine. I've lost a little blood is all. It's nothing, really. (*Pause.*) A mishap. (*Pause.*) Clean-shaven . . .

JOHN: God, what's wrong with you?

ROBERT: There's nothing wrong with me. My hand slipped. (*Pause.*) I'm tired. That's all. I'm tired. (*Pause.*) I need to rest. We all need rest. We all need rest. It's much too much. It's just too much. I'm tired. (*Pause.*) You understand? I'm *tired*.

JOHN: Well, I'm calling you a doctor.

ROBERT: No. You're not. No. Please. I'm only tired. I'm going to go home. I'm only tired. We think we see things clearly when we haven't enough sleep. But we do not. I've cut my-self. I've dirtied up the basin. (*Pause.*) I'm going to go home now.

JOHN: I'll come home with you.

ROBERT: No. Thank you. I'll get home alone. I only have to rest now. Thank you. (*Pause.*) But thank you all the same.

JOHN: I'll take you home.

ROBERT: What? No. I think I'm only going to sit here for a mo-ment. (*Pause.*) I'll be all right. I'll be all right tomorrow. I'll be my old self. I'm all right *now*. (*Smiles.*) (*Pause.*) I'm only going to rest a moment . . . and then I'll go home.

JOHN *looks to* ROBERT *for a moment, then exits.* ROBERT *remains onstage alone for a moment, then slowly exits.*

Scene 26

Backstage, after a show.

ROBERT: I loved the staircase scene tonight.

JOHN: You did?

ROBERT: Just like a poem.

Pause.

JOHN: I thought the execution scene worked beautifully.

ROBERT: No. You *didn't.*

JOHN: Yes. I did.

Pause.

ROBERT: *Thank* you. Getting cold, eh?

JOHN: Yes.

ROBERT (*to himself*): It's getting cold. (*Aloud*) You know, my father always wanted me to be an actor.

JOHN: Yes?

ROBERT: Always wanted me to be . . .

Pause.

JOHN: Well! (*Crosses and picks up umbrella.*)

ROBERT: It's raining?

JOHN: I think it will. You got a fag?

ROBERT: Yes. Always wanted me to be.

ROBERT *hands* JOHN *a cigarette.*

JOHN: Thank you.

ROBERT: Mmm.

JOHN: Got a match?

ROBERT: You going out?

JOHN: Yes.

ROBERT: Where? A party?

JOHN: No. I'm going with some people.

ROBERT: Ah.

JOHN: You have a match?

ROBERT: No.

JOHN *hunts for a match on the makeup table.*

JOHN: Are you going out tonight?

ROBERT: I don't know; I suppose so.

JOHN: Mmm.

ROBERT: I'm not eating too well these days.

JOHN: No, eh?

ROBERT: No.

JOHN: Why?

ROBERT: Not hungry.

JOHN *picks up matchbook, struggles to light match.*

I'll get it.

JOHN: Do you mind?

ROBERT: No.

ROBERT *takes matchbook and lights* JOHN's *cigarette.*

JOHN: Thank you.

    Pause.

ROBERT: A life spent in the theatre.

JOHN: Mmm.

ROBERT: Backstage.

JOHN: Yes.

ROBERT: The bars, the house, the drafty halls. The penciled scripts . . .

JOHN: Yes.

ROBERT: Stories. Ah, the stories that you hear.

JOHN: I know.

ROBERT: It all goes so fast. It goes so quickly.

    Long pause.

JOHN: You think that I might borrow twenty 'til tomorrow?

ROBERT: What, you're short on cash?

JOHN: Yes.

ROBERT: Oh. Oh. (*Pause.*) Of course. (*He digs in his pocket. Finds money and hands it to* JOHN.)

JOHN: You're sure you won't need it?

ROBERT: No. No, not at all. No. If I don't know how it is, who does?

    Pause.

JOHN: Thank you.

ROBERT: Mmm. Goodnight.

JOHN: Goodnight.

ROBERT: You have a nice night.

JOHN: I will.

ROBERT: Goodnight.

> JOHN *exits. Pause.*

Ephemeris, ephemeris. (*Pause.*) "An actor's life for me."

> ROBERT *composes himself and addresses the empty house.* HE *raises his hand to stop imaginary applause.*

You've been so kind . . . Thank you, you've really been so kind. You know, and I speak, I am sure, not for myself alone, but on behalf of all of us . . . (*composes himself*) . . . all of us here, when I say that these . . . *these* moments make it all . . . they make it all worthwhile.

> *Pause.* JOHN *quietly reappears.*

You know . . .

> ROBERT *sees* JOHN.

JOHN: They're locking up. They'd like us all to leave.

ROBERT: I was just leaving.

JOHN: Yes, I know. (*Pause.*) I'll tell them.

ROBERT: Would you?

JOHN: Yes.

> *Pause.*

ROBERT: Thank you.

JOHN: Goodnight.

ROBERT: Goodnight.

> *Pause.*

> JOHN *exits.*

ROBERT (*to himself*): The lights dim. Each to his own home. Goodnight. Goodnight. Goodnight.

V